Railroad Accident Report

**Derailment of Northeast Illinois Regional
Commuter Railroad Train 519 in
Chicago, Illinois
October 12, 2003**

NTSB/RAR-05/03
PB2005-916303
Notation 7615A
Adopted November 16, 2005

National Transportation Safety Board
490 L'Enfant Plaza, S.W.
Washington, D.C. 20594

National Transportation Safety Board. 2005. *Derailment of Northeast Illinois Regional Commuter Railroad Train 519 in Chicago, Illinois, October 12, 2003.* Railroad Accident Report NTSB/RAR-05/ 03. Washington, DC.

Abstract: About 4:38 p.m. central daylight time on October 12, 2003, westbound Northeast Illinois Regional Commuter Railroad (Metra) train 519 derailed its two locomotives and five passenger cars as it traversed a crossover from track 1 to track 2 near Control Point 48th Street in Chicago, Illinois. The train derailed at a recorded speed of about 68 mph. The maximum authorized speed through the crossover was 10 mph. There were about 375 passengers and a crew of 3 onboard. As a result of the accident, 47 passengers were transported to eight local hospitals. Of these, 44 were treated and released, and 3 were admitted for observation. Damages from the accident exceeded $5 million.

The safety issues discussed in this report are the adequacy of the locomotive engineer's performance, training, and qualifications, and the lack of a safety redundant system to address train crew performance deficiencies.

As a result of its investigation, the National Transportation Safety Board issued safety recommendations to the Federal Railroad Administration and the Northeast Illinois Regional Commuter Railroad (Metra). The Safety Board also reiterated a previously issued safety recommendation to the Federal Railroad Administration.

Contents

Executive Summary

About 4:38 p.m. central daylight time on October 12, 2003, westbound Northeast Illinois Regional Commuter Railroad (Metra) train 519 derailed its two locomotives and five passenger cars as it traversed a crossover from track 1 to track 2 near Control Point 48th Street in Chicago, Illinois. The train derailed at a recorded speed of about 68 mph. The maximum authorized speed through the crossover was 10 mph. There were about 375 passengers and a crew of 3 onboard. As a result of the accident, 47 passengers were transported to eight local hospitals. Of these, 44 were treated and released, and 3 were admitted for observation. Damages from the accident exceeded $5 million.

The National Transportation Safety Board determines that the probable cause of the derailment of Northeast Illinois Regional Commuter Railroad (Metra) train 519 was the locomotive engineer's loss of situational awareness minutes before the derailment because of his preoccupation with certain aspects of train operations that led to his failure to observe and comply with signal indications. Contributing to the accident was the lack of a positive train control system at the accident location.

In its investigation of this accident, the Safety Board examined the following safety issues:

- Adequacy of the engineer's performance, training, and qualifications, and

- Lack of a safety redundant system to address train crew performance deficiencies.

As a result of its investigation of this accident, the Safety Board makes safety recommendations to the Federal Railroad Administration and the Northeast Illinois Regional Commuter Railroad (Metra). The Board also reiterates a previously issued safety recommendation to the Federal Railroad Administration.

Factual Information

Accident Synopsis

About 4:38 p.m. central daylight time[1] on October 12, 2003, westbound Northeast Illinois Regional Commuter Railroad (Metra) train 519 derailed at a speed of about 68 mph as it traversed a crossover from track 1 to track 2 in the vicinity of Control Point (CP) 48th Street[2] in Chicago, Illinois. The entire train, consisting of two locomotives and five passenger cars, derailed. The maximum authorized speed through the crossover was 10 mph. There were about 375 passengers and a crew of 3 onboard. As a result of the accident, 47 passengers were transported to eight local hospitals. Of these, 44 were treated and released, and 3 were admitted for observation. Damages from the accident exceeded $5 million.

Accident Narrative

The crew of the accident train went on duty at 1:41 p.m. on October 12, 2003, in Joliet, Illinois. The crew of three, consisting of an engineer, a conductor, and an assistant conductor, had been called from the extra board[3] for this Sunday assignment. The crew was scheduled to operate a commuter train on two round trips between Joliet and Chicago. The train was designated 518 for the eastbound trip to Chicago and 519 for the westbound return trip back to Joliet.

Before the departure from Joliet to Chicago, the engineer received a track warrant from the dispatcher authorizing his train to occupy the track between Joliet and Chicago. Because maintenance-of-way crews were working along portions of tracks 1 and 2, the track warrant also included a Form B track bulletin that granted protection to the track workers. In addition, a Form D identified a portion of track 1 as out of service.

Train 518 departed Joliet with two locomotives and five cars at 2:24 p.m. for the 41-mile trip to Chicago. The train was operated in the push mode.[4] It arrived at the Chicago LaSalle Street Station at 3:42 p.m., about 2 1/2 minutes ahead of schedule. The crew characterized the trip as uneventful.

---

[1] All times in this report are central daylight time.

[2] CP 48th Street is Metra's name for the signal location near 47th Street in Chicago.

[3] An *extra board* employee does not have an assigned job but is called as necessary either to substitute for a regular employee who is unavailable for duty or to serve as a crewmember on an unscheduled assignment.

[4] In the *push mode*, the motive power is at the rear of the train, which is operated from a control cab car on the head end. A train in the *pull mode* is operating conventionally. This "push-pull" configuration eliminates the need to turn or switch equipment at the end of each run, thus allowing quicker turnarounds at terminals.

The crew had about a 47-minute layover to prepare for the scheduled 4:30 p.m. departure of train 519 from Chicago to Joliet. The crew ate lunch near the terminal and prepared to depart. The conductor said that the crew participated in a "general job briefing before departure concerning which cars were being operated [and] what [they] expected to do at Gresham, which has a smaller platform." The engineer asked the train dispatcher about any changes or voids on his track warrants; he was told that none existed.

Train 519 departed Chicago, milepost (MP) 0.0, on schedule[5] at 4:30 p.m.[6] with the same equipment and consist as train 518, but the two locomotives were now at the lead in the pull mode. The engineer was alone at the controls of the lead locomotive. The conductor and assistant conductor were in the coaches to collect tickets. The first scheduled station stop was Gresham, MP 9.8, at 4:47 p.m. (See figure 1 for a diagram of the Metra route between Chicago and Joliet.)

Train 519 was routed onto track 1 as it left Chicago. The engineer was required to radio the foreman of the work crew before entering the protected section of track, located west of Gresham, to arrange for safe passage of the train, as he had done on his eastbound trip. The Form B restriction was in effect from 8:00 a.m. until 5:00 p.m. on both track 1 and track 2. In addition, the Form D indicated that a portion of track 1, just west of Gresham, was out of service until 7:00 p.m. The train received a clear signal[7] as it entered track 1. The engineer successfully conducted the required rolling air brake test. At 4:33:45 p.m., the train reached 16th Street, which is the site of a crossover with a 25-mph maximum speed. The engineer said that he was somewhat surprised that his train was not routed through the 16th Street crossover from track 1 to track 2, as it had been on previous weekend trips. He said he was also thinking about the track crew that might still be working on track 1 near (west of) Gresham, and he decided he would call the foreman of the track crew when he reached 53rd Street, MP 5.3.

After train 519 departed the Chicago LaSalle Street Station, the dispatcher realized that track 1 would not be available for train 519 all the way to Gresham, as he had planned, because of work equipment that was authorized to be on track 1 east of Gresham.[8] Therefore, train 519 would need to use a crossover from track 1 to track 2.

---

[5] The crew used the same warrant it had used from Joliet to Chicago.

[6] Times and speeds in this section were taken from data downloaded from event recorders on the train's two locomotives.

[7] The Safety Board acquired the data logs recorded by field signal equipment to obtain the clock times, track conditions, switch positions, and signal indication codes. A *clear signal* indicates that the train is permitted to proceed at track speed. It will not be required to reduce speed to diverge from one track to another, nor will it have to stop before reaching the second signal in advance of any *clear signal*. Generally, *clear* is the most favorable signal.

[8] At 2:51 p.m., the dispatcher issued, via telephone, the track and time limits (Track and Time Form 10.3.2) to a track foreman located at Gresham, MP 9.8. Limits were granted to permit track equipment occupancy on track 1 between Englewood, MP 6.7, and Gresham, until the foreman released these limits.

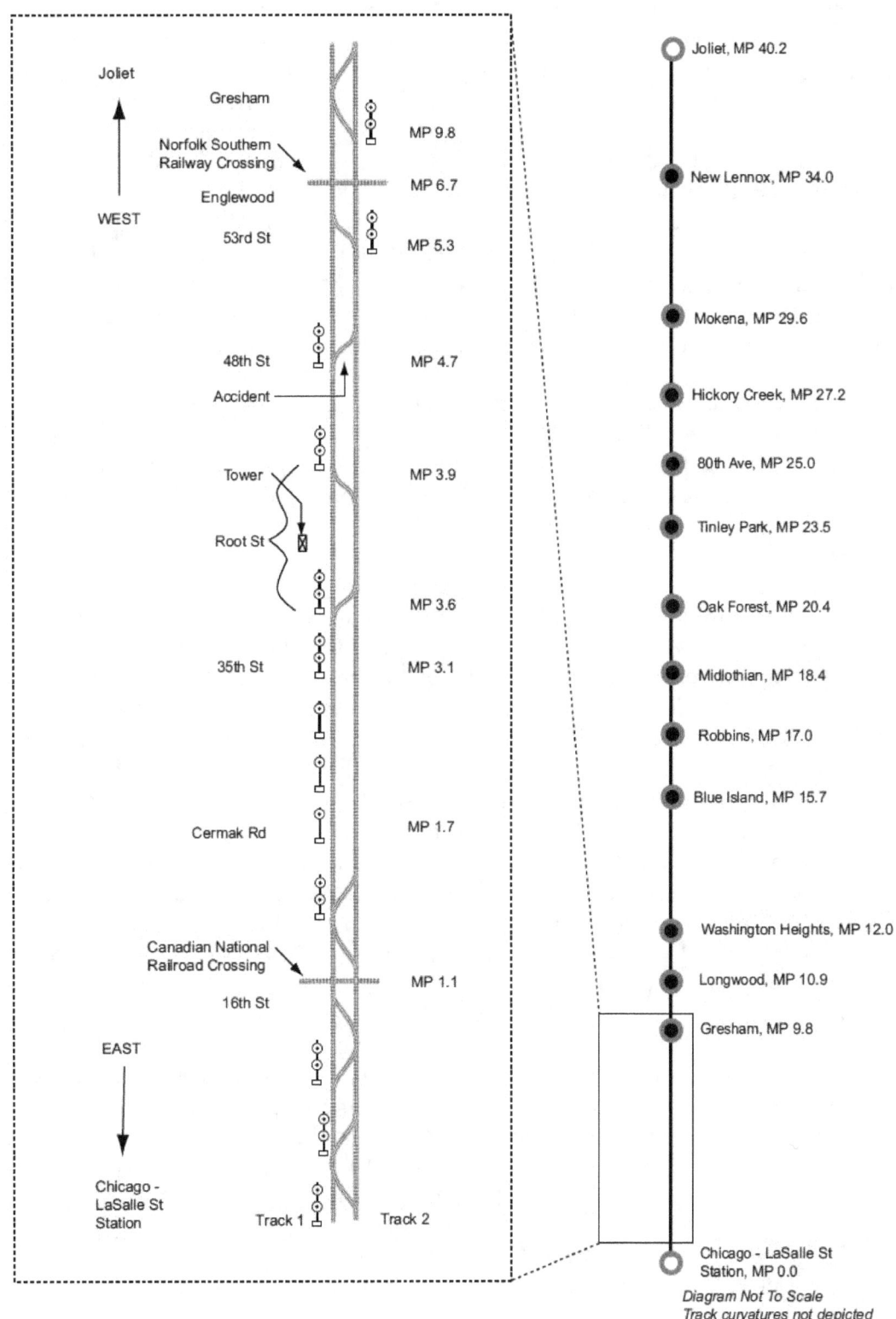

Figure 1. Metra route between Chicago and Joliet.

The dispatcher said that he decided to use CP 48th Street because using other locations closer to the Chicago LaSalle Street Station would have required him to stop the train to allow time for signal safety protocols. The lining of the route at CP 48th Street, including both the crossover and signal displays, was started at 4:32:11 p.m. When the lining was completed at 4:36:12 p.m., the train was located about 8,600 feet east of the crossover.

At 4:34:57 p.m., the train reached the signal at Cermak, MP 1.7; the engineer said that he saw a clear signal. He also said that he saw clear signals ahead and began scanning various locomotive gauges and attending to his speed. At 4:36:28 p.m., the train approached the signal at 35th Street, MP 3.1. He said that he was concerned that he was still operating on track 1 and that the work crew might still be working on the same track near Gresham. The engineer said that he reexamined his track warrant and track bulletin, wondering, "Is there something else here I missed on my track bulletin?"

The engineer said that as the train continued toward the next signal, near Root Street, he was thinking, "Why [is the dispatcher] keeping me on [track] 1?" He said he concluded that since he had already passed two interlockings without crossing over, he would probably be routed to cross over at Gresham. At this time, the train was traveling 56 mph, 1 mph over the 55-mph maximum timetable authorized speed for passenger trains at that location.

At 4:37:01 p.m., the train reached the signal at the beginning of Root Street, MP 3.6, which was displaying a clear indication. At this point, the track begins a 2,100-foot dip. As the engineer entered the dip, he adjusted his throttle to decrease the train speed in accordance with the 50-mph speed restriction across the dip. He said that as his train traveled through the dip, he was watching the rear of his train, anticipating accelerating when the rear of the train cleared the dip. Once the entire length of the train was completely out of the dip, the head end was close to the signal at the end of Root Street interlocking, MP 3.9. This signal displayed approach diverging. By rule, the engineer, upon receiving this signal, was to "proceed prepared to advance on diverging route at next signal and through the turnout [CP 48th Street] at maximum authorized speed [10 mph]." Instead of slowing down, the engineer increased the throttle from the 4th to 8th position. He said that he also checked various gauges, including his speedometer. He said he then checked the time, which was the last action he said he remembered performing before the train entered the crossover at CP 48th Street, MP 4.7.

The CP 48th Street signal at the crossover was displaying diverging clear, requiring the engineer to "proceed on diverging route at prescribed speed [10 mph] through turnout." He had not attempted to slow or stop the train. The train, traveling 68 mph, derailed at the crossover. The accident occurred 4.65 miles and about 8 minutes after the train left the Chicago LaSalle Street Station.

At the time of the derailment, the conductor and assistant conductor were still collecting tickets from the estimated 375 passengers.[9] Emergency brakes applied

---

[9] Because the train had just left the station and tickets were still being collected, the exact number of passengers onboard at the time of the accident could not be determined.

automatically as the train derailed. The locomotives and cars separated. Both locomotives and all five of the passenger cars derailed, striking a Metra passenger-equipment wash building on track 6 at Metra's 47th Street Yard. The lead locomotive overturned onto its right side, facing south. The trailing locomotive derailed upright, facing north adjacent to the lead locomotive. The derailed passenger cars remained upright and parallel to the track structure. (See figure 2 for a photograph of the derailed locomotives and figure 3 for a photograph of the derailed passenger cars.)

Figure 2. The lead locomotive (on its side) and second locomotive at their final resting positions.

After the accident, the engineer used the radio to transmit "Emergency, emergency, emergency. Train down at 47th Street." He said that he did not remember a response. He said that he remembered that there was smoke in the locomotive and that he climbed up to get to the side door to exit the overturned locomotive. He said that once he found the conductor, he told him, "I'm not sure what happened. I saw a clear and I continued to believe I was on all clears because that's what I saw."

Upon notification of the accident, the Chicago Office of Emergency Management and Communications initiated the Chicago Fire Department's first response at 4:41 p.m. The initial response consisted of two engines, two hook and ladders, and a battalion chief. The first units arrived on scene at 4:44 p.m. Firefighters extinguished a fire in the lead locomotive, and a hazardous materials support unit was called because of a locomotive fuel tank leak. Nineteen ambulances would eventually respond to the scene. Passengers were already getting off the derailed coaches when the first units arrived. The train's locomotives and cars were searched and evacuated. Between 40 and 45 people were transported from the scene by ambulance. The remaining passengers were transported by bus from the scene. A command post was established to the west of the incident. Emergency responders remained on scene until 8:00 p.m.

Figure 3. All five passenger cars derailed but remained upright. The trucks from the lead locomotive dislodged (foreground).

Postaccident Inspections and Tests

Investigators conducted postaccident inspections of train equipment, track, and signals. No mechanical conditions of the equipment were identified as factors preventing compliance with the operational requirements of the train. Locomotive event recorders documented responses to the engineer's throttle and brake manipulations. Track structures in the accident area were determined to be consistent with Federal Railroad Administration (FRA) regulations. Damage at the point of derailment was consistent with an overspeed derailment. Investigators, through inspection and review of signal event recordings, determined that the signals displayed aspects for crossing over from track 1 to track 2 at CP 48th Street at the time of the accident.

At the time of the accident, the temperature was 68° Fahrenheit, and visibility was 10 miles. No witness, including the engineer, noted a weather-related visibility impediment. The investigators did not find any environmental factors, including the sun's position, structures, or a locomotive cab windshield condition that would have obstructed the engineer's view of the signal aspects. During postaccident interviews, the engineer stated that he had no difficulties seeing or distinguishing the signal aspects. Following the accident, investigators, who rode a similar train to the accident site at about the same time of day, noted that they had good signal visibility from inside the locomotive cab, which allowed them to see two or three signal aspects in front of the train. The engineer stated that his first indication of a problem was when the train hit the crossover switch. Sight-distance testing conducted, at night, after the accident revealed that the diverging clear signal was visible and discernable beginning about 7,900 feet (and about 1 minute 30 seconds) before the crossover point.

The engineer had two cell phones with him during the trip—one was his personal phone and the other was provided by Metra. Phone records showed that neither had been used during the accident trip. No other electronic devices were found at the scene, and the locomotive radio had not been used from the time the train departed Chicago until it derailed.

Metra Profile

Metra operates 700 weekday trains over its 545-mile system and provides 300,000 passenger trips daily and 80 million passenger trips annually. Metra has 12 routes. Four of those routes are operated under purchase-of-service agreements with the Union Pacific Railroad and the BNSF Railway Company (BNSF). The remaining eight routes are operated by Metra employees. The Metra equipment fleet includes 130 locomotives and more than 1,000 passenger cars. (See figure 4 for a map of Metra's system.)

The accident occurred on the Rock Island District, Joliet Sub District, one of the eight routes operated by Metra employees. The district encompasses the territory from the Chicago LaSalle Street Station to the Joliet Union Station.

Trains receive authority to enter and occupy the centralized traffic control limits from signal indications. Each train must receive a track warrant at its initial station unless otherwise instructed by the train dispatcher.

Metra's Locomotive Engineer Training Program

General

According to Metra's *Locomotive Engineer Training Program* manual, the training program for Metra engineers is a 40-week course that combines classroom studies and field training with hands-on operation of commuter trains under the supervision of qualified Metra engineers. Candidates spend the first 90 days under the guidance of the supervisor and assistant supervisors of locomotive engineers. Classroom training includes the following topics: signal systems, operating and safety rules, mechanical and electrical systems, physical characteristics of Metra districts, and emergency procedures.

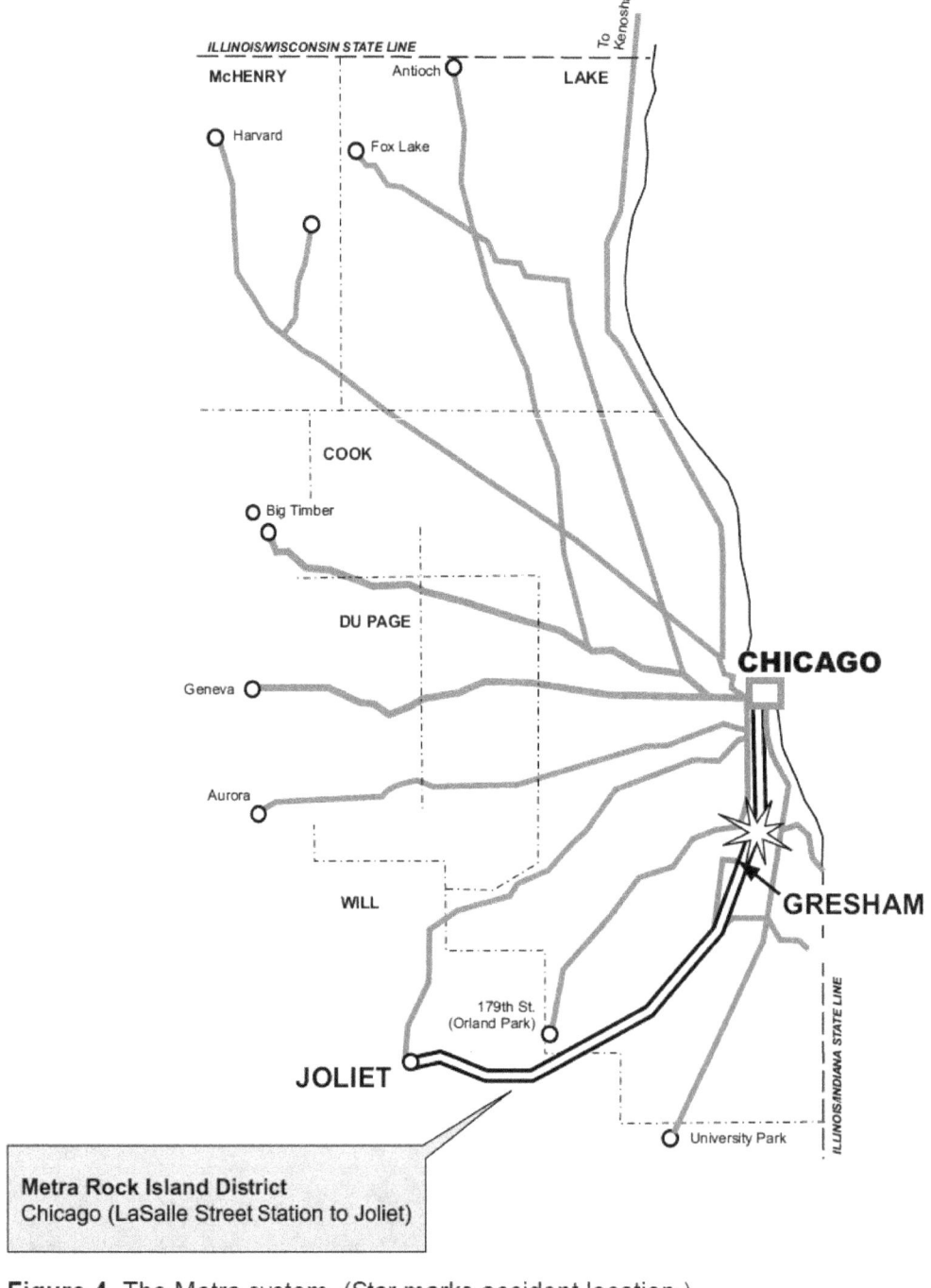

Figure 4. The Metra system. (Star marks accident location.)

The training for new employees typically included time on a locomotive simulator.[10] Engineer trainees spent 7 hours operating trains on the simulator and spent additional time observing other trainees on the simulator. The simulator utilized a predefined sequence of events and, therefore, did not allow the interactive altering of trip events that would challenge a trainee's acquired knowledge and skill or teach the development of task strategy management in operating a train safely during atypical situations. For example, it could not simulate signal changes, grade crossing malfunctions, signal malfunctions, train delays, or restrictions not specified in writing.

Upon successful completion of the initial 90-day training period, the candidates are assigned to "engineer trainers" (who are qualified Metra engineers) on specific districts. According to Metra, the engineer trainer serves as both an instructor and a mentor, with the goal of developing a high level of professionalism and aptitude in students. When this phase of the training is completed, the candidates take a certification exam. Upon completion of the program and achieving a satisfactory score on the certification exam, the students become qualified as engineers and are assigned to districts. According to Metra, the engineer trainees (candidates) must demonstrate proficiency on the signal system aspects and their operational meanings by achieving a 100 percent rating on that part of the examination.

Training of the Accident Engineer

The 37-year-old engineer first qualified as a locomotive engineer with BNSF in May 2000; however, he was not used by BNSF as an engineer on a regular basis.

On June 18, 2001, the engineer joined Metra as an assistant conductor trainee on the Rock Island District. He became an assistant conductor on July 16, 2001, and a week later was transferred to the Metra Electric District. In February 2002, he entered Metra's locomotive engineer training program. The 40-week program was suspended on September 25, 2002, and the engineer continued to work as an assistant conductor. He took a military leave of absence from the railroad from January 3 to February 5, 2003. Upon the engineer's return to Metra on February 5, he reentered the training program, which had been restarted, but left a few days later for another military leave. He returned from his second military leave on June 16, 2003, and resumed his training as a student engineer.

Because his military deployment coincided with the 10th week of his engineer training, which was when the class used simulators, he missed the simulator training. According to Metra, when he returned from his military deployment, he made 10 training trips. These trips were closely monitored by Metra officials. Based on his performance during these training trips, he was allowed to rejoin his engineer training class, which had moved into the on-the-job-training, revenue train service, phase of the program. To help compensate for the training components he had missed during his military absence, Metra assigned him to operating switch engines in the yard. He received his engineer's certification on July 21, 2003.

---

[10] The simulator training was conducted at the Illinois Institute of Technology Research Institute in Chicago, which no longer offers such training. Metra representatives told the Safety Board that Metra is investigating alternative methods of providing simulator training.

Engineer's Experience, Work Schedule, and Health

Experience

The engineer, as a trainee, made about 112 round trips between Chicago and Joliet under the supervision of an on-board qualified engineer.[11] The engineer recalled operating the newer model locomotives only a few times after taking a new locomotive orientation class on June 17, 2003; he did not recall ever operating the new locomotives as multiple units. He had no record of any disciplinary actions for operating rules violations.

In the 2 1/2 months between his certification and the accident, the engineer worked 24 days as a certified engineer for Metra commuter trains.[12] He initially alternated between the Southwest and Rock Island Districts before being transferred to the Milwaukee District, where he worked 11 assignments. He had been reassigned to the Rock Island District 2 days before the accident. (See table 1.)

Table 1. Engineer's Assignments (July 25-October 11, 2003)

District	Work Period	Number of Days Worked
Southwest	July 25	1
Rock Island	July 26-30	2
Southwest	August 1	1
Rock Island	August 5-14	3
Southwest	August 15	1
Rock Island	August 16-18	3
Milwaukee	August 19-October 6	11
Rock Island	October 10-11	2

While working commuter service, he typically made two round trips per day, although on some assignments in which trips were not to the end of the line, he made more. After he became a qualified engineer who operated alone, he had made 23 westbound trips from Chicago to Joliet.

Work Schedule

On October 10, 2003, 2 days before the accident, the engineer had worked from 6:12 a.m. to 6:00 p.m. The day before the accident, October 11, he worked from 7:24 a.m. until 5:51 p.m. He said that on the night before the accident, he had gone to bed no later than 9:30 p.m. He said that he awoke feeling rested. He also said that 6 hours is a normal amount of sleep for him.

Health

The engineer reported being in good health. He had passed his last company physical examination (vision and hearing) in January 2003 and was allowed to operate a

---

[11] The majority of the trips took place before September 2002, before Metra suspended its engineer training program.

[12] During this period, the engineer also worked in noncommuter service, such as in the yard or on a work train.

locomotive without restrictions. He said that he had not taken any nonprescription medications within the 72 hours before the accident and did not take any prescription medications or illicit drugs.

After the accident, he provided toxicological specimens that were tested for the presence of alcohol and drugs pursuant to 49 *Code of Federal Regulations* Part 219, Subpart C. No drugs[13] or alcohol were identified in either specimen.

Engineer's Description of Operational Concerns

During interviews with Safety Board investigators, the engineer discussed some operational concerns he had had soon after he began the accident trip. These included his uncertainty about the whereabouts of the maintenance-of-way crew, his approach to spotting the train at station platforms, and his unfamiliarity with the train equipment.

Between the time that the engineer became qualified and the day of the accident, he worked on the Rock Island, Milwaukee, and Southwestern Districts, with most of his time split between the Milwaukee and Rock Island Districts. When working on the Milwaukee District, he generally used older locomotives. The Rock Island District had some new locomotives that were longer and heavier and had greater horsepower (3,600 versus 3,200) than the older locomotives that the engineer operated on the Milwaukee District. In addition, the controls on the new locomotives were on a desktop stand instead of on a stand on the engineer's left-hand side.

On the Rock Island District, the engineer usually operated a train with one locomotive. The train he operated on the day of the accident used two of the new locomotives. He said that he believed this was the first time he had operated a train with two new locomotives coupled together.[14] On the accident trip, he said, he had noticed that the two new locomotives accelerated more quickly than the locomotives on the Milwaukee District. He said that he had checked his speed more frequently than he normally would because his train was "very much quicker" than the trains he typically operated. He also stated that "[the new locomotives] go so fast ... you could find yourself 5 to 10 miles ... above the speed limit if you're not paying attention." He stated that the train was picking up speed in throttle position 3 to the point that he subsequently needed to apply braking.

---

[13] Substances tested for included cannabinoids, cocaine, opiates, amphetamines, methamphetamines, phencyclidine, barbiturates, and benzodiazepines.

[14] The two locomotives (MP36PH-3S) were the newest type of locomotive Metra uses in passenger service.

Other Information

Requirements for Engineers to Communicate Signals

On February 20, 1996, the FRA, in response to two fatal train accidents,[15] issued Emergency Order No. 20, Notice No. 1, (EO20) to reduce the risks that train passengers and crews face under certain operating conditions. EO20 was aimed at commuter and intercity passenger operators and freight railroads, where push-pull passenger operations are conducted. The order states in part:

> FRA concludes that certain current conditions and practices on commuter and intercity passenger railroads pose an imminent and unacceptable threat to public and employee safety. Of greatest concern are push-pull and [multiple unit[16]] MU operations lacking the protection provided by cab signal, automatic train stop, or automatic train control systems.[[17]]

EO20's applicability for push-pull operations is as follows:

> With regard to cab car forward and [multiple unit] MU operations over territory lacking at least cab signals, the immediate need is to ensure that signal indications are followed. FRA believes that certain operating rules, already in place on many railroads, will assist engineers in remembering and adhering to signal indications. One rule will require that signal indications for an approach or less favorable than an approach be called out by the engineer as they are seen. A designated crewmember elsewhere in the train will acknowledge the communication and, in the absence of an appropriate response to a restrictive indication that has been communicated, take action to ensure the appropriate response. This will serve as a simple device to help the engineer remember to abide by signal indications and will add safety redundancy by involving other crew members in responsibility for safety with regard to compliance with signals.

In response to this order, Metra issued Special Instruction 5.16,[18] directing that a Metra engineer who observes an approach or less favorable indication must orally

---

[15] (a) National Transportation Safety Board, *Employee Fatality, National Railroad Passenger Corporation, Secaucus, New Jersey, November 27, 1996*, Railroad Accident Report NTSB/RAR-97/01 (Washington, DC: NTSB, 1997). (b) National Transportation Safety Board, *Collision and Derailment of Maryland Rail Commuter MARC Train 286 and National Railroad Passenger Corporation AMTRAK Train 29 Near Silver Spring, Maryland, February 16, 1996*, Railroad Accident Report NTSB/RAR-97/02 (Washington, DC: NTSB, 1997).

[16] A *multiple unit* (MU) is a passenger train with carriages that have their own motors, either diesel (DMUs) or electric (EMUs), and do not need to be hauled by a locomotive.

[17] In an automatic *cab signal* system, the signal indication is transmitted to and displayed in the engineman's compartment or locomotive cab. An *automatic train stop* is a trackside system that works in conjunction with equipment installed on a locomotive to automatically apply the brakes and stop the train should the engineer not acknowledge a restrictive wayside signal within 30 seconds of passing it. An *automatic train control* is a system that enforces signal and some civil speed restrictions either by applying the brakes of a speeding train to slow it to the speed required by a restricted signal indication or by applying a full-service brake until either the train stops or the engineer operates the controls to reduce the train speed.

[18] Special Instruction 5.16 does not apply where the maximum authorized speed does not exceed 30 mph or where an automatic cab signal system is in place.

communicate the signal indication to a crewmember anywhere on the train or to a rules-qualified employee in the engine control compartment. Each transmission must be acknowledged by the designated crewmember.

Neither the FRA's emergency order nor Metra's special instruction required the train 519 engineer to communicate to crewmembers the last two signals (approach diverging and diverging clear) encountered before the derailment; these signal indications are more favorable than an approach signal indication.

Further, as part of this accident investigation, investigators noted that EO20 allows railroads to specify yard or terminal limits within which engineers are exempt from the order to call out signals. The terminal area for this line, designated by Metra, extended from the Chicago LaSalle Street Station to the Root Street Tower, which is almost 4 miles from the station. There are eight signals between the Chicago yard and the Root Street Tower that are never called out, regardless of their indications, because they are within Metra's defined terminal area. Metra officials told investigators that

> The territory between Chicago and Root Street was selected because of the already heavy volume of radio traffic involving scheduled train movements between Chicago and 47th Street Coach Yard. It was felt that adding the Emergency Order No. 20 signal calling into this territory could result in confusion from conflicting transmissions and be detrimental to safety.

Safety Redundancies

Metra's locomotive and cab car fleet, including train 519, have in-cab signal equipment that can be utilized on about 152 miles of the 545-mile Metra system. However, no wayside cab signal equipment was ever installed between the Chicago LaSalle Street Station and MP 15, along the route between Chicago and Joliet that includes the accident site. Wayside cab signal equipment is installed on this route from MP 15 to MP 40, Joliet.

Simulator Training in Rail Industry

The Safety Board reviewed the practices of some large railroads to understand the industry's approach to training engineers on task-management skills. The Board found that, to the extent these skills are reinforced through training, such reinforcement is typically done during the engineer trainee's supervised rides. During these rides, the supervisor, typically a road foreman, generates hypothetical situations for the trainee to manage while operating the train. Simulator training, for many of the railroads surveyed, predominately emphasizes developing fundamental train handling skills, and the engineer trainee receives little or no exposure to situations requiring the simultaneous management of multiple tasks.

Postaccident Actions

In the 2 1/2 months between his certification and the day of the accident, the engineer had been assigned to a number of districts. The variation in assignments was consistent with Metra's then-current policy of filling vacant positions with engineers from the extra board or from the bottom of the seniority roster. Since the accident, Metra has modified its practice of rotating newly certified engineers among districts. The present rule states that a newly promoted engineer will be held on an assigned extra board until the employee has obtained 70 starts, including those instances in which the employee is called out of turn.

Analysis

The Accident

Postaccident inspection of the accident train and wayside signal system revealed no defects that would explain the failure of the Metra train 519 engineer to slow his train in preparation for the 10-mph crossover near CP 48th Street. The accident occurred during daylight hours and in clear weather. Signal visibility testing conducted after the accident revealed that the approach diverging and the diverging clear signals would have been visible and discernable from the locomotive cab well in advance of reaching the signals. The accident train was traveling well over the maximum authorized crossover speed when it derailed upon reaching the crossover switch from track 1 to track 2.

The train was traveling approximately 68 mph at the time of the derailment and there was no evidence that it had slowed before reaching the crossover. In postaccident interviews, the engineer stated that he had observed a clear signal when he was going through Cermak with additional clear signals along his line of travel on track 1, and that he had no difficulty seeing or distinguishing the signal aspects. He stated that his first indication of a problem was when the train hit the crossover switch.

General

The investigation determined that the train equipment, tracks, and signal system had all operated as designed. Recorded data from the locomotive event recorder and the wayside signal system revealed no anomalies. Environmental conditions and signal visibility at the time of the accident were adequate. The engineer was not using either of the cell phones he had in his possession. The postaccident toxicological testing for all crewmembers was negative. Therefore, the Safety Board concludes that the mechanical condition of the train, the track structure, the signal system, environmental conditions, cell phones, and drugs and alcohol were not factors in this accident.

The engineer's most critical task was to observe wayside signals and comply with signal indications; had he done so, the accident would not have happened. Therefore, the Safety Board attempted to determine what might have caused the engineer to fail to comply with two critical and consecutive wayside signals.

Engineer's Management of Operational Tasks

The Safety Board examined the engineer's account of the events leading up to the accident and his ability to manage the tasks he faced during the accident trip. The investigation also focused on his exposure to nonroutine operations and his previous experience operating the train equipment. Neither of these factors, in and of themselves, was abnormal or unmanageable by the engineer.

The engineer stated that he was surprised when he passed 16th Street without crossing over from track 1 to track 2. He had expected to be crossed over because he usually ran on track 2 during weekend service. He was also concerned about the whereabouts of the maintenance-of-way work crew, which he knew had been near track 1. He told investigators that his concerns prompted him to devote additional time and attention to scrutinizing his paperwork. However, the routing of the train and separating the train from work crew activity are the responsibilities of the train dispatcher. Instead of continuing to review his paperwork trying to understand why his train was being routed on track 1, the engineer could have contacted the train dispatcher by radio to discuss his concerns.

The engineer stated that after passing 16th Street, he exited a curve, came out on straight track, and saw that the signal at Cermak was clear with clear signals ahead as far as he could see. He stated that he therefore felt comfortable that he had time to make some random safety checks, so he checked his gauges, speed, and track warrant. The engineer stated that he was visualizing his trip and thinking that he would want to call the foreman of the work crew upon reaching 53rd Street, so that he would have plenty of time to slow his train before reaching the area where they were working.

When an engineer changes territories, he often confronts unfamiliar equipment. An engineer on the Milwaukee District, for example, operates trains consisting of one or two older locomotives. On the Rock Island District, he is likely to operate a train consisting of one or two new locomotives, as the accident engineer did. The new locomotives have greater horsepower, respond differently to braking, and have different operating control stands, all of which can be complicating factors to an engineer who is unaccustomed to these differences. Because the accident engineer found the accident train to be "quicker" than those to which he was accustomed, he stated that he referred to the speedometer more frequently than usual as he regulated his speed. The locomotive event recorder indicates that the throttle and braking actions by the engineer were appropriate and that the train was operated at normal speeds until it passed the approach diverging signal at the end of the Root Street interlocking.

None of the fundamental tasks (train handling, signal recognition, and operating rules) faced by the engineer on the day of the accident was beyond his capabilities. However, when his belief that he was operating on clear signals was coupled with his unresolved concerns about the location of the work crew, when he would be crossed over, and other tasks, his ability to operate the train safely was affected.

During postaccident interviews, the engineer indicated that when he saw multiple clear signals ahead he felt that he had some time to focus his attention elsewhere. Although much of his workload was self-imposed, the engineer demonstrated what often happens to someone under a high workload:[19] he increasingly focused on a particular part of the workload to the detriment of his handling of the overall situation. The engineer's excess attention to certain operating concerns, including the location of a maintenance-of-way work crew, where his train would be crossed over, and the regulation of his train speed, likely compromised his ability to maintain situation awareness,[20] or an overview of all safety-critical tasks. The Safety Board, therefore, concludes that the cumulative operating concerns of the engineer likely diverted his attention from the safety-critical task of observing and complying with signal indications.

The Safety Board has investigated other railroad accidents in which the loss of situational awareness was a factor. For example, in its investigation of the collision of an Amtrak train with a Maryland Rail Corporation (MARC) train in Baltimore, Maryland,[21] the Safety Board concluded that a factor in the accident was the engineer's unfamiliarity with the equipment. Specifically, the Amtrak engineer, with about 6 months of operating experience over the territory, had a train that was pulled by two locomotives of a type she had never operated. In addition, she had had limited experience operating locomotives as multiple units. As the engineer was approaching Baltimore station, she became overly concerned with and focused on maintaining her speed; as a result, she did not see either the cab or the wayside signals indicating that she should stop. She continued past the signals and collided with a southbound MARC train near the station.

The Safety Board determined that the probable cause of the accident was

> The Amtrak engineer's loss of situational awareness in the moments before the collision because of excess focus on regulating train speed, which led to a failure to comply with the signal indications. Contributing to the accident was the engineer's lack of familiarity with and proficiency in the operation of the diesel-electric locomotives assigned for the trip....

Developing Task Management Strategies

On the day of the accident, the engineer was confronted with a number of tasks that he should have handled more effectively. Training programs should help prepare students for "real-world" situations and teach them how to prioritize conflicting tasks effectively.

---

[19] The concept of *workload* is the interface between the demands of the task and the resources or effort of the operator. During work overload situations, task demands continue to increase, and errors may result because of the operator's inability to cope with the information rates imposed by the environment. See B.M. Huey and C.D. Wickens, eds., *Workload Transition: Implications for Individual and Team Performance* (Washington, DC: National Academy Press, 1993).

[20] *Situation awareness* is generally defined as a person's perception of the elements in the environment within a volume of time and space, comprehension of their meaning, and projection of their status in the near future. See M.R. Endsley, "Design and Evaluation for Situation Awareness Enhancement," *Proceedings of the Human Factors Society, 32nd Annual Meeting* (Santa Monica, CA, 1988) 97-101.

[21] National Transportation Safety Board, *Collision of Amtrak Train No. 90 and MARC Train No. 437, Baltimore, Maryland, June 17, 2002*, Railroad Accident Brief NTSB/RAB-03/01 (Washington, DC: NTSB, 2003).

One way that Metra attempted to prepare trainees was to have them use locomotive simulators; however, the engineer in this accident did not have simulator training because he was on a military deployment. Although simulators can help prepare engineers to operate trains safely under both normal and abnormal situations, the simulator training Metra's engineers took utilized a predefined sequence of events and, therefore, did not allow interactive altering of trip events that can challenge a trainee's knowledge and skills or teach the development of task strategy management during atypical situations. Therefore, even if the engineer had taken the simulator training, it is unlikely that it would have appreciably affected his performance leading up to the accident.

The aviation community recognizes that each pilot is responsible for managing multiple concurrent tasks (flying the aircraft, navigating, searching for traffic).[22] Both research and accident investigations have shown that often pilots make mistakes not because they are under a work overload, but because they fail to monitor concurrent tasks in a timely manner. Interruptions, distractions, or preoccupation with one task to the detriment of another task are problems identified in numerous Safety Board accident reports. Some accidents were caused by pilots or crews who were preoccupied or distracted by "head-down" tasks, such as tending to paperwork or resolving a problem. Therefore, effective flight training goes beyond acquisition of basic piloting or "stick and rudder" skills and provides the trainee with opportunities to manage both normal and challenging situations, including realistic interruptions, distractions, and concurrent task demands.

Ambiguous problems for which the proper response is not obvious often cause pilots the most difficulty.[23] In an emergency, such as a fire or an engine failure, for which a clear course of action is indicated, crewmembers tend to perform well. They do less well and sometimes neglect even the most basic elements of safe operation when they must spend time and attention on resolving an ambiguous problem. Consequently, much of the aviation industry has incorporated the concept of situational awareness in its pilot training and aircraft simulator scenarios to include both clear-cut and ambiguous problems. Crews learn from reviewing videotapes of their responses how well they managed, particularly whether they became fixated on a problem to the point that they left "nobody minding the store."

Simulators are often used to help flight crews develop task management strategies—the processes by which pilots manage the many tasks that must be done concurrently.[24] The training teaches the crew how to allocate its attention to the different functions when an abnormality increases the workload.[25]A strategy involves monitoring, scheduling, and allocating the tasks and task resources. Such a strategy is particularly

---

[22] K. Dismukes, *Lessons from Aviation: Memory, Skilled Human Performance, and All-too-human Error* (Moffett Field, CA: NASA Ames Research Center, 2002).

[23] C. Bovier, "Situation Awareness, Key Component of Safe Flight," *Flying Careers* January (1997).

[24] K. Funk, I. Colvin, J. Wilson, C. Suroteguh, and R. Braune, *Cockpit Task Management* (Oregon State University and NASA Ames Research Center, 2000).

[25] P. Schutte and A. Trujillo, "Flight Crew Task Management in Non-normal Situations," *Proceedings of the Human Factors and Ergonomics Society 40th Annual Meeting, 1996,* (Santa Monica, CA: Human Factors and Ergonomics Society, 1996) 239-243.

important in managing an abnormal situation, which requires the crew to devote more time and attention to the function related to the cause of the situation.

In surveying some large railroads, the Safety Board found that a trainee's task management skills are typically reinforced during supervised rides, if at all. Those railroads that use simulators do so primarily to develop train handling skills, not to prepare trainees to cope with situations requiring them to manage tasks simultaneously. Accidents can result not only from poor management of emergency situations, but also from a crew's failure to manage routine tasks and normal workload. Using locomotive simulators to present trainees with simultaneous operational challenges that they may face in the field can develop a trainee's ability to prioritize tasks and build confidence, thus preparing the engineer to operate safely even while coping with unusual or unexpected circumstances. The Safety Board concludes that training an engineer to develop task management skills may provide strategies that will allow the engineer to operate safely when encountering a high workload or atypical situations. The Safety Board believes that the FRA should develop guidelines for locomotive engineer simulator training programs that go beyond developing basic skills and teach strategies for effectively managing multiple concurrent tasks and atypical situations.

The Safety Board recognizes that the FRA will need time to develop simulator training guidelines that would be universally applicable to all railroads. The Safety Board believes that Metra does not need to wait for the FRA to complete its efforts, but rather, Metra should begin to use locomotive engineer simulator training to go beyond developing basic skills and teach strategies for effectively managing multiple concurrent tasks and atypical situations.

Calling Out Signal Indications

FRA's EO20 requirement for calling out certain signal indications is intended to add safety redundancy by involving other crewmembers in helping to ensure compliance with wayside signals in the absence of the protection provided by cab signals, automatic train stop, or an automatic train control system. In this situation, the approach diverging and diverging clear signals required the accident engineer to slow the train to 10 mph so that it could negotiate the crossover. The Safety Board understands that these signals did not meet FRA's definition of signal indications that must be called out.

Metra had designated several miles of track near where the accident occurred as a terminal area that was exempt from the requirement for signal callouts. Within this defined terminal area, there is no wayside cab signal equipment, positive train control, or other safety redundant system to compensate for human errors. Further highlighting the potentially severe consequences of failing to comply with signal indications through this area is the existence of a freight railroad crossing less than 2 miles from Chicago.

The accident engineer's most critical task was to observe and comply with wayside signal indications; however, he stated that when he saw multiple clear signals ahead he felt comfortable having time to focus his attention elsewhere. If he had been required to call out these upcoming signal indications over the radio, then he likely would not have perceived the situation prior to the accident as an opportunity to divert his attention elsewhere; instead he likely would have been monitoring his location relative to each signal in preparation for making each callout. Therefore, calling out all signal indications would have better focused the engineer's attention on the safety-critical task of complying with the wayside signal system. Further, a crewmember hearing the engineer radio "approach diverging" would have expected the train to slow, so when it accelerated, a crewmember might have radioed the engineer for clarification or intervened. Although the calling out of signal indications does not prevent missed signals or incorrectly perceived called signals, the Safety Board concludes that had the engineer been required to call out all signal indications over the radio, there would have been a greater likelihood that he or another crewmember would have responded to the wayside signals. The Safety Board believes that Metra should require its train crews to call out all signal indications over the radio, including clear signals, at all locations that are not equipped with automatic cab signals with enforcement or a positive train control system.

Currently, CSX Transportation (CSX) and the Norfolk Southern Railway Company (NS) require train crews to call all signal indications over the radio. Both CSX and NS have push-pull passenger operations on their systems: the Virginia Railway Express (VRE) and MARC. Accordingly, both VRE and MARC call out all signal indications when operating on these railroads. Further, several other railroads require train crews to call out signals under various circumstances and conditions. The Safety Board believes that the FRA should require train crews to call out all signal indications over the radio, including clear signals, at all locations that are not equipped with automatic cab signals with enforcement or a positive train control system.

Positive Train Control

The Safety Board is concerned about the safety of railroad operations when backup systems are not available to intervene if a train crew operates a train improperly or fails to comply with wayside signals. Safety Board railroad accident investigations over the past three decades have shown conclusively that the most effective way to avoid train-to-train collisions is through the use of a positive train control system that will automatically assume some control of a train when the train crew does not comply with the requirements of a signal indication. In fact, positive train control has been on the Safety Board's Most Wanted Transportation Safety Improvements list since the list was developed in 1990.[26]

In its investigation of the April 23, 2002, collision of a BNSF freight train with a Metrolink passenger train near Placentia, California,[27] the Safety Board concluded that

---

[26] The Safety Board developed the Most Wanted Transportation Safety Improvements list, consisting of previously issued safety recommendations, to bring special emphasis to the safety issues the Board deems most critical. The list is reviewed, revised, and reissued as needed, or at least annually.

[27] National Transportation Safety Board, *Collision of Burlington Northern Santa Fe Freight Train With Metrolink Passenger Train, Placentia, California, April 23, 2002,* Railroad Accident Report NTSB/RAR-03/04 (Washington, DC: NTSB, 2003).

Had a fully implemented positive train control system been in place on the Burlington Northern Santa Fe's San Bernardino Subdivision at the time of the accident, the system would have intervened to stop the freight train before it could enter into the track area occupied by Metrolink 809, and the collision would not have occurred.

The Safety Board has investigated numerous train accidents in which the probable cause or contributing cause was the inattention of the crewmembers to wayside signals. In its investigation of the head-on collision of two freight trains near Kelso, Washington,[28] the Safety Board concluded that

> passive wayside light signals are not wholly adequate for preventing accidents because they do not always capture a train crew's attention or provide any safety redundancy or back-up when crewmembers misinterpret, disregard, or fail to pay attention to a signal.

The Safety Board also urged the railroad industry to recognize that human vigilance alone cannot prevent accidents. In fact, previous Board investigations identified many factors affecting a crew's performance and its ability to comply with signals, including multiple distractions,[29] talking on a cell phone,[30] dense fog,[31] crew inattention,[32] crew fatigue (or falling asleep) due to irregular work and sleep cycles,[33] sleep disorders,[34] and prescription medications causing drowsiness.[35] After each of these investigations, the Safety Board stated that had the accident location had a positive train control system with a collision-avoidance component, the system could have detected that the engineer was not responding appropriately to the signal indications. After this detection, the positive train control system would have stopped the train.

---

[28] National Transportation Safety Board, *Head-On Collision and Derailment of Burlington Northern Freight Train with Union Pacific Freight Train, Kelso, Washington, November 11, 1993*, Railroad Accident Report NTSB/RAR-94/02 (Washington, DC: NTSB, 1994).

[29] NTSB/RAR-97/02.

[30] National Transportation Safety Board, *Collision of Two Burlington Northern Santa Fe Freight Trains Near Clarendon, Texas, May 28, 2002*, Railroad Accident Report NTSB/RAR-03/01 (Washington, DC: NTSB, 2003).

[31] National Transportation Safety Board, *Collision Involving Three Consolidated Rail Corporation Freight Trains Operating in Fog on a Double Main Track near Bryan, Ohio, January 17, 1999*, Railroad Accident Report NTSB/RAR-01/01 (Washington, DC: NTSB, 2001).

[32] NTSB/RAR-03/04.

[33] National Transportation Safety Board, *Collision and Derailment Involving Three Burlington Northern Freight Trains near Thedford, Nebraska June 8, 1994*, Railroad Accident Report NTSB/RAR-95/03 (Washington, DC: NTSB, 1995).

[34] National Transportation Safety Board, *Collision of Two Canadian National/Illinois Central Railway Trains near Clarkston, Michigan, November 15, 2001*, Railroad Accident Report NTSB/RAR-02/04 Washington, DC: NTSB, 2002.

[35] National Transportation Safety Board, *Collision and Derailment of Union Pacific Freight Trains MPRSS-21 and AJAPRB-21 at Des Plaines, Illinois, October 21, 2002*, Railroad Accident Brief NTSB/RAB-04/04 (Washington, DC: NTSB, 2004).

The Safety Board concludes that this Metra accident is another in a series of accidents that could have been prevented had there been a positive train control system at the accident location. Such a system could have detected the engineer's lack of response to signal indications and then could have either stopped the train or slowed it to a speed at which it could have safely moved through the crossover. The Safety Board believes that Metra should install a positive train control system on its commuter train routes.

The most recent positive train control related safety recommendation issued to the FRA was a result of the Safety Board's investigation of the train collision involving three freight trains in Bryan, Ohio,[36] and it was reiterated following the Placentia, California, accident:

R-01-6

Facilitate actions necessary for development and implementation of positive train control systems that include collision avoidance, and require implementation of positive train control systems on main line tracks, establishing priority requirements for high-risk corridors such as those where commuter and intercity passenger railroads operate.

This recommendation is currently classified "Open–Acceptable Response."

The FRA issued a final rule that became effective on June 6, 2005, that establishes performance-based standards for processor-based signal and train control systems. According to the FRA, this rule will facilitate the introduction and implementation of train control systems by providing technology-neutral performance-based criteria for determining safety. Additionally, the FRA provided the Safety Board with information about several positive train control development projects that it continues to fund, and the FRA participated in the Positive Train Control Symposium sponsored by the Board in March 2005. However, the Board remains concerned about the lack of positive train control systems on many passenger train routes and is convinced that these systems provide the best approach to reduce human-error accidents. Therefore, the Safety Board reiterates Safety Recommendation R-01-06 to the FRA.

---

[36] NTSB/RAR-01/01.

Conclusions

Findings

1. The mechanical condition of the train, the track structure, the signal system, environmental conditions, cell phones, and drugs and alcohol were not factors in this accident.

2. The cumulative operating concerns of the engineer likely diverted his attention from the safety-critical task of observing and complying with signal indications.

3. Training an engineer to develop task management skills may provide strategies that will allow the engineer to operate safely when encountering a high workload or atypical situations.

4. Had the engineer been required to call out all signal indications over the radio, there would have been a greater likelihood that he or another crewmember would have responded to the wayside signals.

5. The October 12, 2003, Metra accident is another in a series of accidents that could have been prevented had there been a positive train control system at the accident location.

Probable Cause

The National Transportation Safety Board determines that the probable cause of the derailment of Northeast Illinois Regional Commuter Railroad (Metra) train 519 was the locomotive engineer's loss of situational awareness minutes before the derailment because of his preoccupation with certain aspects of train operations that led to his failure to observe and comply with signal indications. Contributing to the accident was the lack of a positive train control system at the accident location.

Recommendations

As a result of its investigation of the October 12, 2003, derailment of Metra train 519 in Chicago, Illinois, the Safety Board makes safety recommendations as follows:

New Recommendations

To the Federal Railroad Administration:

Develop guidelines for locomotive engineer simulator training programs that go beyond developing basic skills and teach strategies for effectively managing multiple concurrent tasks and atypical situations. (R-05-9)

Require train crews to call out all signal indications over the radio, including clear signals, at all locations that are not equipped with automatic cab signals with enforcement or a positive train control system. (R-05-10)

To Northeast Illinois Regional Commuter Railroad (Metra):

Use locomotive engineer simulator training to go beyond developing basic skills and teach strategies for effectively managing multiple concurrent tasks and atypical situations. (R-05-11)

Require your train crews to call out all signal indications over the radio, including clear signals, at all locations that are not equipped with automatic cab signals with enforcement or a positive train control system. (R-05-12)

Install a positive train control system on your commuter train routes. (R-05-13)

Recommendation Reiterated in This Report

The National Transportation Safety Board reiterates the following safety recommendation to the Federal Railroad Administration:

<u>R-01-6</u>

Facilitate actions necessary for development and implementation of positive train control systems that include collision avoidance, and require implementation of positive train control systems on main line tracks, establishing priority requirements for high-risk corridors such as those where commuter and intercity passenger railroads operate.

BY THE NATIONAL TRANSPORTATION SAFETY BOARD

MARK V. ROSENKER
Acting Chairman

ELLEN ENGLEMAN CONNERS
Member

DEBORAH A. P. HERSMAN
Member

Adopted: November 16, 2005

Deborah A. P. Hersman, Member, filed a concurring statement on November 16, 2005.

Notation 7615A

Member HERSMAN, concurring:

Although I concur with the findings and with the recommendations contained in this report, I would have preferred the report to include recommendations that would provide interim safety solutions that railroads and FRA can implement relatively quickly while work continues on the development of PTC and on new regulations.

Despite the many resources invested by the Federal government and the rail industry to develop technologies, like PTC, that provide safety overlays for controlling the movement of trains, widespread implementation of these systems is still many years away, particularly for publicly-funded commuter operators such as Metra that operate over various railroad properties. It is reasonable to recommend that Metra should implement a PTC system on its routes at some time in the future; it is unreasonable to expect that this commuter rail operator will be able to do so in the near term. In the meantime, there may be other technologies that are more practical for Metra to install to achieve greater safety protection while it moves toward the implementation of a more complete train control system like PTC (*e.g.,* additional route miles outfitted for operation of the cab signals, automatic train stop (ATS), or other redundant technologies, some of which are already operational on certain routes or portions of routes operated by Metra).

In that same vein, the recommendation to FRA to require train crews to call signal indications should also include a recommendation that the agency take immediate steps to tighten loopholes in Emergency Order 20. This emergency order is designed specifically for the protection of push-pull and multiple unit operations on commuter and intercity passenger railroads, such as Metra, where trains operate at speeds faster than 30 mph over routes where there are no operable cab signals, ATS or ATC. In part, the emergency order requires a crew member in the controlling cab to call signals to another crew member elsewhere on the train. Application of the emergency order is limited to areas outside yard or terminal limits as set by the railroad. Railroads may be setting such limits beyond what was originally envisioned, excluding many miles of their operations. FRA should review existing yard and terminal limits to determine if they are appropriate and do not dilute the intent of the emergency order. Emergency Order 20 is further limited to only those signals that require the train to stop or operate at restricted speed at the next signal. It does not apply to signals indicating a diverging clear, as in the case of this accident, even though the diverging signal required the train to slow down significantly, from 68 mph to 10 mph, as it approached the crossover. The result is that Emergency Order 20, despite its purpose of protecting train movements of commuter and intercity passenger operations by requiring engineers to call signals, was not applicable in the train movement immediately preceding this accident.

The Board is recommending in this report that FRA require all railroads to call out all signals at all locations that are not equipped with PTC or with automatic cab signals with enforcement. While this recommendation may improve rail operational safety, it calls for a new Federal regulation that must be implemented through the lengthy rulemaking process. In the meantime, commuter and intercity passenger operations carrying thousands of passengers each day would continue to pose a risk to their passengers from signals missed by train crews. (In fact, a similar accident to this one has already occurred earlier this year at this same location.) I would have preferred that this report recommend to FRA that while it pursues the rulemaking, it also revise Emergency Order 20 to require train crews on commuter and intercity passenger operations to call signals at all locations where the signal indicates that the train must be slowed significantly before the next signal.

Furthermore, the recommended rulemaking to require calling all signals would apply to freight railroads, as well as commuter passenger operations, all across the country. Although it seems intuitive that such a requirement would have a positive impact on the attentiveness of the engineer, there currently is no hard data to scientifically support the theory. In fact, I have reservations about the effectiveness of calling signals on passenger operations where the conductors or other crew members are not in the locomotive cab, because 1) they cannot see the signals to confirm or challenge the signals called by the engineer, and 2) they often are occupied with other duties in the passenger cars. I would have liked the recommendations to include a suggestion that FRA collect data on railroads' compliance with, and the safety effectiveness of, Emergency Order 20. The data could then be used to justify the signal-calling requirement on a much broader segment of railroads.

Finally, to compliment the recommendations, I would have preferred the probable cause to include additional contributory causes. It may be true that the lack of PTC contributed to this accident, but so did the lack of other redundant operational safety measures, such as improved training and oversight of crew compliance with signals, signal calling by the crew and operational cab signals. The probable cause would have been more accurately stated if it said that contributing to the accident was the lack of PTC and any other redundant operational safety measures that enhanced crew compliance with the signals.

Appendix A

Investigation

The National Response Center notified the National Transportation Safety Board of the accident about 7:00 p.m. on October 12, 2003. The Safety Board immediately dispatched a Chicago-based investigator and a Washington D.C.-based investigator to the scene. Two additional investigators were assigned once it was determined that their expertise was needed. No Board Member participated in the on-scene investigation.

No hearings or depositions were held in conjunction with this accident.

The Northeast Illinois Regional Commuter Railroad, the Federal Railroad Administration, the Brotherhood of Locomotive Engineers, the United Transportation Union, the Brotherhood of Railroad Signalmen, and the Illinois Commerce Commission were all parties to this investigation.